Book of
POOLE QUAY
and the
Waterfront

Andrew Hawkes

Previous Publications

The Pride of Poole, 1688-1851
An Album of Old Poole
Mansions and Merchants of Poole and Dorset
Brownsea Islander
Poole and World War II
A Portfolio of Old Poole
Ebb-Tide at Poole
History of the Town of Poole, 1839 (facsimile)
The Sydenhams of Poole (booklet)
Art in Poole and Dorset
Victorian Poole
Poole after World War II 1945-1953
D-Day Poole (booklet)
The Spirit of Poole 1953-1963

Lifeboatmen Never Turn Back
Schools of Old Poole
Poole's Pride Regained 1964-1974
Poole Was My Oyster
Hengistbury Head - The Whole Story
I Was There
For Nature Not Humans
The Royal Motor Yacht Club 1905-2005 (private publication)
A Winsome Place
A Pint of Good Ale
Up On Hill
Brownsea Island (facsimile of Van Raalte 1906)

ISBN 978-/-873535-875
Production by Graphic Editions Ltd, Poole. Printed by Ashley Press, Poole, Dorset.

Publications by the same Author

Memories of Old Poole – The Quay
Memories of Old Poole – The Old Town
Memories of Old Poole – Poole High Street
Memories of Old Poole – Poole Park
Memories of Old Poole – Parkstone
Memories of Old Poole – Sandbanks
Memories of Old Poole – Brownsea Island
Memories of Old Poole – Canford Cliffs
Memories of Old Poole – Broadstone
Illustrated Poole & Bournemouth
Lifeboatmen Never Turn Back
Brownsea Island
A Pint of Good Poole Ale

The Town Cellars and the Great Quay, circa 1485.

Acknowledgements

Cover picture: *Poole Quay from The Shipwrights Arms* by Bernard Gribble (1872 - 1962), Borough of Poole Museum Service

Great Quay - Graham Smith and Poole Museum

Shellfish Stalls on the Quay - Frank Henson

Lifeboat Harmer in the Slipway - Simon Wills

Pictures have also be used from the collections of

Barbara and Ernest Bristowe, Ernest Coney and Sidney Batting

Otherwise all pictures including postcards come from the *Andrew Hawkes Poole Picture Archive.*

There may be pictures used which are still in copyright to the original photographer that have not been credited. If so the author apologises and would appreciate information.

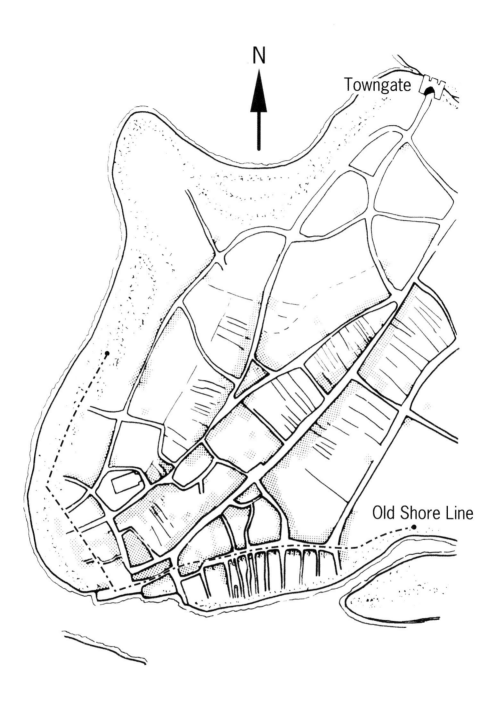

N

Towngate

Old Shore Line

Foreword

Poole Quay can be regarded as the town's beating heart, the basic reason for its existence and has always made a huge contribution to its economy and social life. This book makes use of hundreds of photographs to reveal how the Quay and the waterfront have changed over the last two centuries.

In earliest times the town of Poole was almost an island, nearly surrounded by water with only boggy wetland areas and tidal dykes dividing it from the mainland. This made it an ideal place for a town to become established as it was easily defended. To the south west of the town there was a deep channel separating it from Hamworthy which was a smaller area of land, again almost surrounded by water. All the waterfront areas were beach, some of it hard shingle and other, more sheltered ones were soft mud.

The first port in Poole harbour was established by the Romans after the invasion in AD43 at the Hamworthy side of the Little Channel, Little Channel is the stretch of the water downstream of the present Hamwothy Bridge (often incorrectly called today Poole Bridge). The shore of the east side of Hamworthy would have been hard shingle and the water flow from the upstream bay of Holes Bay (or Longfleet Bay) would have kept the shore line from silting up. The spit of land would have been easy to defend and the water behind it would provide a sheltered haven.

In Saxon times there were two or more ports in the harbour. Poole was the largest which served the town and the estate of Great Canford. The second was at the town of Wareham, which is served by two rivers, thus giving easy access to the rest of Dorset. Other ports on the southern side of the harbour were mostly landing places nearest to the hamlets along the Isle of Purbeck shore, mostly only suitable for shallow draft vessels, such as ferryies.

Although Wareham was a busy Saxon port, the rivers at Wareham were silting up due to agricultural activities further inland. This caused earth to erode from the land filling the rivers and made them shallow and fast flowing and therefore unsuitable for sea going vessels attempting to make the trip up the river to Wareham, and especially as the draught of vessels became larger, Wareham declined. Poole took the opportunity to provide a safe haven for the larger ships. It had deep, sheltered water, near land and had suitable beaches to build jetties or piles where ships could tie up and take the ground at low tide for loading and unloading. As years went by the ground between the jetties was filled by storage sheds, the jetties became pathways, and later the sheds became warehouses, the jetties became the lanes between them. The layout of these can still be traced in the buildings which front the quay today between Strand Street and the Quay. It has been estimated that up to 40% of the present land mass of Poole below the level crossing is land reclaimed from the sea.

By the 13th century Poole was becoming a popular port and because sea-going vessels were becoming larger, with high sides which made them unsuitable for unloading on a sloping foreshore, these vessels preferred to stay in deeper water, and as the jetties were dependent on the tide and the amount of water needed to float the ships, it was decided that a Quay had to be built alongside the deep water so that ships could lay afloat at all stages of the tide.

A large warehouse was wanted with a building for the taxmen to collect Customs or Taxes on goods being imported and exported, especially after Poole becoming a Port of the Staple.

One built in 1433 is the Town Cellar; this building remains today and although part of it was severed in the nineteenth century to put a road to the quay (Thames Street) it still remains the largest medieval store house in the British Isles. Around the cellar was a possible gate and wall, built to protect the town behind it, and the Quay from the town. There was also a Custom House to control it all; in front of this building was a large flat area where goods could be handled complete with a quayside named the Great Quay of some 240ft (73m), where ships could tie up to at all states of the tide.

In the 15th century, because Poole was now a prosperous town, it attracted foreign merchants who were not averse to turning to piracy to get what they wanted from the town. Also Poole merchants were also renowned for piracy, and this attracted retaliation for their damage on other ports, so another quay was built to the south of the Great Quay. This quay was called the Little Quay and cannon were placed on it to protect the town from foreign invaders and pirates. It soon became known as the Gun Deck, and there was a similar Gun Fort built in stone on the other side at Hamworthy, and another Gun Deck on the harbour shore. Not only were they used for the defence of the town they were used for training of troops to defend the town.

These quays served Poole well until the 16th century. Around this time Poole merchants established trade across the Atlantic to Newfoundland, returning via the Mediterranean. New quays were wanted to serve this trade so the existing one was extended south again in front of the well-established warehouses by the old jetties. This proved successful and other areas around the north side of the town were converted to quayside and became the main quay for shipping.

The Hamworthy side (Ballast Quay) remained mostly unchanged and was used for building, careening and repairing ships. The marsh land was dug out to provide ponds in which timber was stored to be pickled by salt water to give it a longer life and slowly this side was also converted to quayside.

Over the next four hundred years the Quay has been added to as the town has grown to its present size. Various plans have been made in the past to provide deep water quays elsewhere in the harbour but none have were built due to the lack of deep water at the bar of sand that lies off the harbour mouth.

The arrival of railways and later roll-on/roll-off carrying goods in containers has taken the shipping trade away from Poole Quays. A larger quay for cross channel ro-ro trade and passengers has been built to the harbour side of Hamworthy and New Quay has now become the main quay for shipping. It retains a railway connection but is rarely used. The quayside on the Hamwothy side is mainly used for luxury ship building of pleasure vessels, mostly for export.

The Quay on the Poole side is an area now dominated by tourism where ferry boats leave for the island of Brownsea and the beaches of Sandbanks, and trips round the harbour or up to Wareham. Because of the increase of small boat ownership, the quayside area, known as Oyster Bank, off Dolphin Quay (formally Poole Pottery and the old gasworks) has been protected by off shore stone walls and the seabed deepened to provide a boat haven for local people and visiting yachtsmen. The fishermen have been given there own area to keep their boats.

Poole Harbour Commissioners - until 1895 the Quays on the Poole and Hamworthy waterfront came under the control of a Quay Committee of Poole Corporation. This was then a body in the control of often warring politicians fighting for party political power and not dedicated to securing the future of a commercial enterprise, but merely relying on it as a source of revenue to avoid falling into debt again, as it had done in the 1830's. However, the Quay Committee was always the last item on the Council agenda.

As a shallow draught port what it needed to compete with other ports was investment to sustain or, better still, increase its trade by deepening the entrance to the harbour at the bar and dredging the channels although it had extended the Pottery Quay and, rather reluctantly, commissioned a report about a training bank at the Sandbanks entrance.

An Association of Harbour Users was formed, inflamed by increases in quayage rates and particularly by an increase of 1d in rates for clay, a principal export cargo. Under pressure, and after a Sheriff's meeting, a private Bill was forced on the Council to change the constitution.

It was passed by Parliament in 1895, and a more responsive body was created, incorporating harbour interests (there was still a majority of councillors; the Mayor, six councillors and a representative from Wareham) but for the first time there were representatives of landowners, tradesmen, fishermen and the railway. It took over on 9th November 1895. This was a bitter defeat for the Council not least because it passed to the Commissioners newly reclaimed land behind the extended East Quay as well as land at Sandbanks intended to be given to the Council by Lord Wimborne

This constitution survived for many years with slight amendments and Council influence was only diminished to a minority on the trust which now controls the Quays and all marine matters in the harbour (including commercial, recreational and ecology) relatively recently.

Andrew Hawkes

Contents

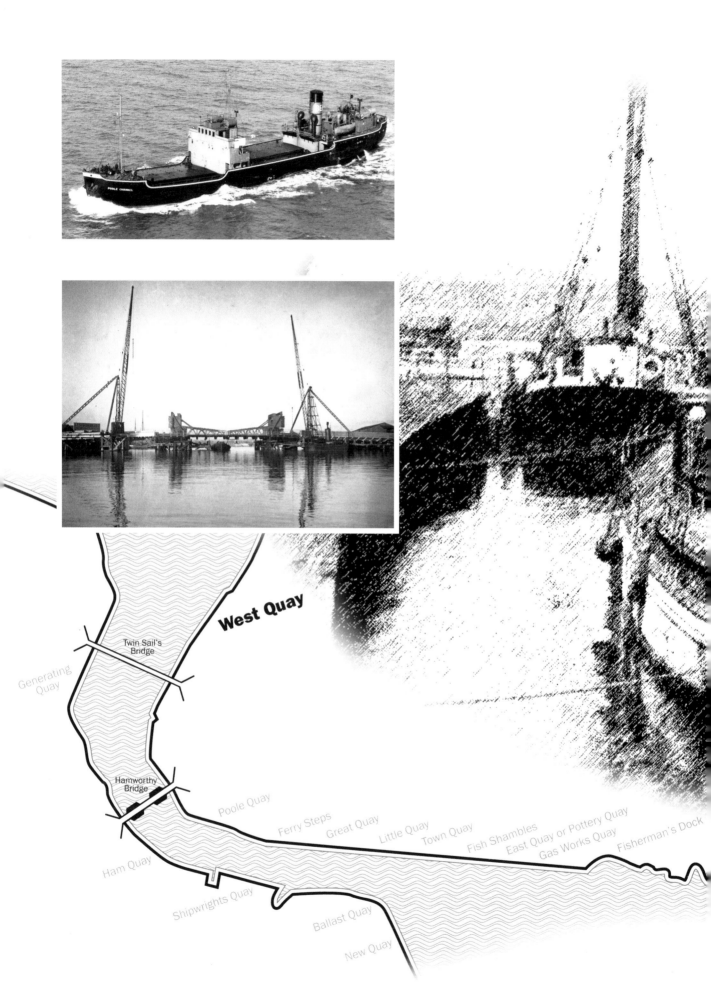

West Quay

Twin Sail's
Bridge

Generating
Quay

Hamworthy
Bridge

Poole Quay

Ferry Steps   Great Quay

Little Quay   Town Quay

Fish Shambles

East Quay or Pottery Quay

Gas Works Quay

Fisherman's Dock

Ham Quay

Shipwrights Quay

Ballast Quay

New Quay

WEST QUAY

Baiter

Back Water Channel, West Quay and Poole from Hamworthy, c1910.

Holes Bay from the air, Back Water Channel and West Quay in the foreground c1910.

Poole from the air, Back Water Channel and West Quay in the foreground c1910. The quays were built here between 1634 and 1751

Back Water Channel and West Quay from the air showing Bolson's shipbuiding yard, soon to become a shipyard again building Lifeboats for the RNLI.

The British Drug House chemical
works c1920.

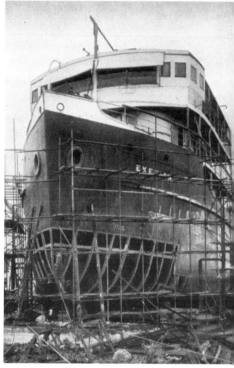

Above: Shuttler's boatbuilding yard,
refitting the Poole Lifeboat.

When Shuttlers Boatbuilding yard
closed it was taken over by Bolson
who started to build landing craft.

Bolson's Ship building yard was able to build ships up to 300 ft in length. In 1940 production was switched to the British Power Boat Company making landing craft.

The Royal Navy Auxiliary ship YC484 on the Bolson building slip. She was to be used for Salvage, Mooring and Boom Defence.

The "SAND SNIPE" launching from Bolson's Ship building yard, previously Shutler's boatbuilding yard.

Before the Poole Generating Station was built the area was known as the Lynpool, used as a mud berth for storing laid-up vessels.Below the 'Mary Walters' of Jersey laid waiting for new instructions

Timber ship has been unloaded into the yard in at West Quay from the Backwater Channel.

Sydenhams & Company Wharf. The "RATHLIN ISLAND" alongside unloading Baltic timber.

Above: The construction of Poole Generating Station started in 1947.

Centre left: The "BOJAN" alongside Tug "WENDY ANN".

Left: Four-masted timber ship uploading at West Quay.

The mud lands where Poole Generating Station was built, and below the steelwork going up.

Bottom: Preparing the site.

Poole Generating Station or Hamworthy Generating Station as it became known opened May 18th 1949, it was built on the mud lands next to Carters pottery. with a new 1000ft wharf , 500ft for unloading coal and 200ft for disposing the ash.

The seawater inlet for cooling, and the foundation piles under the chimneys. The chimneys were built using locally made sand lime bricks.

Poole Generating Station, built from 1947, was originally coal fired, it was later converted to oil. The chimneys were 325ft high with a diameter at the bottom of 27ft tapering to the top at 19ft., the chimneys had removable filters inside, to remove harmful gases and other contaminants.

Above and bottom left: View from Generating Station

The Generating Station had its own fleet of ships to service it.

Top: "POOLE QUAY"

Bottom: After the station was converted to oil the "ESSO POOLE" was a supply ship.

The view from Arne which shows how the chimneys dominated the skyline and were a landmark for sailors.

Below: On 3rd February 1993 the chimneys were demolished; the rest of the building was to follow.

Artist's impression of the first Poole bridge, seen from the Hamworthy side, it was built 1833/5 and was a toll bridge built of wood costing £9000. It was named Hamworthy Bridge.

This is the earliest photograph of the first Hamworthy Bridge taken from Hamworthy quay in the late 1850's. It was opened by Hon. William Francis Spencer Ponsonby, 1st Baron de Mauley, the lord of the Manor of Canford. The bridge could be opened by hand by swinging aside the centre, which let ships pass through.

On 28th January 1895 the waters of Holes Bay froze. When the tide went out, the Ice floes were trapped by the bridge and soon froze solid enough for people to walk across from Hamworthy to Poole.

Above: The Toll House and Mrs Gooden the toll keeper by the gate. The charges were paid to the bridge owners, but they were regulated by an Act of Parliament and were controlled by Poole Corporation.

The second Hamworthy Bridge, was opened in 1885 and was still a toll bridge operated by a private company. It was made to open with two swinging bascules which were opened by hand, to swing in opposite directions to allow ships through. The Bridge was purchased for £16k by the Corporation in 1924 to be demolished to build the third bridge

Above: Laying the foundations of the third Hamworthy Bridge in 1926; the cost was £33,600 and its length 331 feet.

Center: Building the bascule lifting leaves.

Bottom right: Completed bridge in 1927.

Left: Steam Rollers and two fully-laden coal trucks were used to weight test the bridge.

Below: The crowds of people on the Quay watching the performance, and the Mayor retuning from the Hamworthy side. Crowds watching the Mayor, Alderman Herbert Carter, cutting the tape at the the opening ceremony.

King Neptune was the first to sail under the open new bridge.

Closed and open to traffic and fully open
to allow large ships through.

Top right: Hamworthy Bridge. Note the Carter's Tiles Bottle
Kilns in the background.

Opposite: Poole's Twin Sails Bridge from Hamworthy to West
Quay opened in April 2012, at a cost of £37 million.

Twin Sail's
Bridge

West Quay

Generating
Quay

Hamworthy
Bridge

Poole Quay

Ferry Steps   Great Quay

Little Quay   Town Quay

Fish Shambles

East Quay or Pottery Quay

Gas Works Quay

Fisherman's Dock

Ham Quay

Shipwrights Quay

Ballast Quay

New Quay

HAM QUAY

Baiter

Top left: The Railway Yard next to the bridge in 1890 and later 1950's.

Above: The view of Poole Quay from the Railway Yard Quay in 1900.

Opposite page:

Left and right: View from Hamworthy Bridge showing the Railway Yard Quay in the 1950's and 1920's. Newman's yard is in the middle.

Top right: The "GONDOLIER" boats built by Bolson's ready to take passengers round the harbour.

Top centre right: Yacht-building yards between the wars.

Some larger yachts receiving repairs and maintenance before the new season.

The Shipwrights' Arms a waterside public house, on the Hamworthy side of the Quay alongside a ferry landing place.

The Bosun's Locker, the lounge bar.

A Ferry has operated from Ferry Road for hundreds of years; it declined when the first bridge opened. The rights to operate a ferry were last let in 1961. The Shipwright's Arms provided an occasional service in the holiday season, for customers until the public house was closed in 1974. A ferry also ran when repairs were made to the current Hamworthy Bridge.

Many of the pictures taken from the windows and Quay of the Shipwrights Arms were the work of one man, a Mr. Coney who was the friend of Miss Preston, the landlord's daughter, and he was responsible for taking all these pictures in this area.

The largest shipyard on the Hamworthy side was this one. In the 19th century it built ships for Wanhill and later, in the 20th century it became the repair and fitting out yard of Bolson & Son Ltd.

In the 21st century this Hamworthy yard is still involved with shipbuilding and today, Sunseeker builds luxury yachts and ships up to 300ft long, some costing in excess of £10 million pounds, with over 90% being exported. In 2013 it came under Chinese ownership having started as a family owned business.

The barquentine "WATERWITCH" was built by Poole shipwright Thomas Meadus in Poole. The keel was laid in 1868 and completed and launched in November 1871. She became a very well known vessel, principally because she was to be the last British square rigged sailing vessel to sail and carry cargo under the Red Ensign. She was one of the largest wooden ships that could be built in Poole, she was 112ft long with a beam of 25.8ft. weighing 206.26 tones. She is known to have visited Poole, loading clay for Liverpool Docks to be taken to the Midland Potteries. She was reported lost in the Baltic sea, in the autumn of 1944.

Ballast Quay where ships were able to load or off load ballast if departing or arriving without cargo. The aerial picture dates to about 1920.

Above and opposite page: Shows the building of the extension Quay to be named New Quay, in the 1930's.

"WESTERN PRIDE" was withdrawn from service in 1966 and broken up.

Building the crane which would be used to unload and load shipping that would use the new berths alongside the New Quay.

Once built the crane were used to handle all kinds of cargo which included caravans built for export by Bluebird (later BK Caravans), scrap iron, tyres, timber, clay, apples, cement, and anything else that needed to be handled in Poole.

Generating Quay

Twin Sail's Bridge

West Quay

Hamworthy Bridge

Poole Quay

Ferry Steps

Great Quay

Little Quay

Town Quay

Fish Shambles

East Quay or Pottery Quay

Gas Works Quay

Fisherman's Dock

Ham Quay

Shipwrights Quay

Ballast Quay

New Quay

POOLE QUAY

Baiter

Poole Regatta had been held in the harbour from the mid 19th century. The Regatta was held once a year between the Quays. Water Polo was most popular with a rope and buoy rectangle laid out with a goal at each end. Swimming races took place with classes for ladies, men and children and there was a greasy pole with a pillow fight for the energetic lads. Water boxing took place on a pontoon for the ring; the match continued until one was forced into the water. One thing was for certain, all contestants eventually ended up in the water!

Whilst the townspeople had their Regatta between the Quays, rowing skiffs from other towns also had races. They were launched off the beach on the other side of Hamworthy Quay and the races took place from Poole Quay out and round buoys laid off the Main Channel by Stakes Buoy off New Quay, and back again.

This end of the Quay, near the bridge, was used as a storage area where ships could unload directly onto the Quay, also tie up to wait sailing orders or new cargo or crew.

Above: A Paddle steamer, believed to the "PRINCESS", loading guests to be taken to Brownsea Island for the service of consecration of St Marys church in 1854.

Left: Unloading stone for the local building trade in the early 1900's.

Below left: A waggon loaded with grain from Dorchester waits to be loaded for export.

Opposite page top: Unloading Timber from the Baltic.

Opposite page bottom: View from Hamworthy Bridge

Top: Clay from the Purbeck Hills was one of Poole's largest exports. The clay was brought down from the hills to small jetties around the Harbour where it was tipped into barges then towed to Poole. It was then loaded into baskets and tipped into sea-going vessels to be taken mainly to Liverpool where it would be again put in barges and taken to the Midland Potteries.

Below: The Swedish sailing ship "ALBEGE" with a cargo of Scandinavian timber.

Above: Children crabbing on the Quay.

Right: The Quay from Hamside.

Below: An unknown three-masted ship loading clay.

Views from Hamworthy Bridge in the 1950's. The Nissen hut was left from the Second World War when the Navy used it to control shipping in the Harbour.

Views from Hamworthy Bridge in the 1960's. The Nissen hut was then used by the Poole Harbour Commissioners as a store and a hydrographic office, where the hydrographic surveys and tidal surveys was prepared for the new nautical charts of the harbour.

In the background can be seen a new Christopher Hill grain silo. It was demolished in 2011.

Right: During the period after the second World War to the late 1990's this area was used as a safe haven for visiting yachts, and at bank holidays it became very crowded with up to five boats deep laying alongside each other.

Above: The new "WENDY ANN I & II"

Below: The original "WENDY ANN"

With motor boats and yachts, at times the area could come very congested, which could lead to some interesting scenes when the tide changed, when a mooring line broke or insufficient line had been used.

The increasing visiting yachts to Poole Quay, led to the building of marinas in other areas of the harbour.

The visit to Poole, in the mid 1930s' of a quarter-size model of "HMS VICTORY".

Top: Yeatman's Victoria Mill on the Quay, dates back to the early 1700's

Above: Yeatman & Sons 1912 Garrett steam wagonette, one of the first lorries in the Poole area.

Left: Behind Yeatman's Mill is the "Watergate or Archers Steps" said to be part of the original Town Wall built in the time of King Richard III.

The "LADY OF AVENEL" on Poole Quay. Built in Cornwall in 1874 as a trading schooner, trading in cod from Newfoundland and fruit from the Azores. It is said she was also involved in the slave trade. She held the record for having sailed to the most northern point, in 1925, in an Arctic expedition. In 1933 she was converted to a private yacht.

When the Second World War was declared the "LADY OF AVENEL" was laid up for the duration off Brownsea Island, but the area had to be cleared and she was moved to Holes Bay where she fouled her anchor and sank on top of it; she became a total loss.

The Ship's Wheel; a dining room table was saved, the binnacle was also saved and is in Poole Museum and her masts became flag poles, one at the Redcliffe YC at Wareham and the other outside Carter's Tiles in Hamworthy.

Generating
Quay

Twin Sail's
Bridge

West Quay

Hamworthy
Bridge

Poole Quay

Ferry Steps

Great Quay

Little Quay

Town Quay

Fish Shambles

East Quay or Pottery Quay

Gas Works Quay

Fisherman's Dc

Ham Quay

Shipwrights Quay

Ballast Quay

New Quay

GREAT QUAY

Baiter

By 1688 there was more or less a continuous quay from 40ft off the eastern end of St James' Church to the Town Cellars. Further east was mud land as far as Baiter. In 1750 Dr. Pocock wrote "There are several Quays at the end of the town and on each side of the merchants' yards go to the water and some have quays to them."

Ferry Steps is on the eastern end of the Great Quay, where ferries from Hamworthy and other parts of the harbour landed.

This part of the Quay was used as a mooring place for ships whilst waiting new sailing orders and cargoes.

Bottom right: "Sailors' Return" opposite Ferry Steps. This Inn was a passage house where people could wait for the ferry to take them to all parts of the Harbour.

Ferry Steps in the 1950's - 1970's the area was used as a mooring place for the Poole Bay pleasure boats

Left: The two original boats, "POOLE BELLE" and "BOURNEMOUTH BELLE". Note the railway splits into two lines here.

Bottom left: When the original "POOLE BELLE" was sold the name transferred to a new "POOLE BELLE".

Bottom right: The "LADY BETTY" waiting to take a trip round the harbour.

The Great Quay was the first Quay to be built at Poole in the 13th and 14th centuries very much on the line of the present Thames Street (along the line of St. Clements Wall to Strand Street). The quayside has been rebuilt on reclaimed land to the south several times since.

By the 19th century there were three public houses, a sail maker and a ship's chandler. Also the Town House, Town Cellar or King's Warehouse, and the Custom House.

H & A Burden & Co, Ships Chandler, Coal Merchant and Haulage Contractor.

Henry Burden owned a traction engine which was used to transport heavy loads all around the town and area.

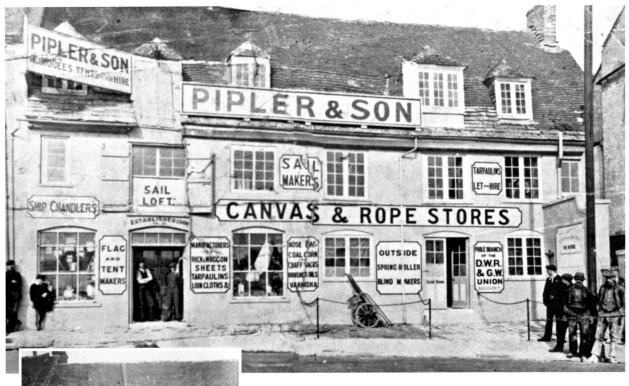

The business of Pipler & Son was founded in 1866 as a sail maker supplying Rope, Canvas, Sails, Tents, Marquees, Shop Blinds, Flags and anything else made of canvas. The business still remains today as a general yachtsman's chandlery.

The Great Quay was Poole's first Quay; a document of 1558 gives its length of 240 feet as long.

It was built when ships became larger and no longer wished to take the ground when handling cargo.

Originally built in 1727 as the "Town House", a meeting place for the town's merchants and ships masters' where general news could be heard and recorded and merchants could buy and sell from the ship owners. In 1822 the building upstairs was extended by adding the colonnade and the building became the Harbour Office where the Harbour Master controlled shipping in the Harbour until the move to the former Poole Yacht Club premises in Hamworthy, near the ferry terminal.

About 1300 this building was built on the Great Quay, and is known today as the Town Cellar. Originally it was called the "Woolhouse" or the "Kings Hall" for storage of wool and staple goods. When it was built it was it was 120ft long and is one of the best preserved examples of a Woolhouse in Great Britain. In the 19th century the building was divided into two portions when Thames Street was created. The western portion is behind the Harbour Office is used as a hall for the King Charles public house, whilst the eastern end is Poole's Local History Centre. Next door to the Cellar was the Ship Inn.

Opposite page, Top right: Enjoying the sun outside the Town Cellar in the 1940's.

Right: The Quay Pump, the only fresh water pump on Poole Quay. The quality of water was never good enough to be drinking water but used to supply water for animals. All drinking liquid for shipping was taken on board in barrels as beer, as beer stayed fresh.

Far right: Market traders selling vegetables and fresh fruit, about 1890.

This Custom House built in 1813, as the previous Custom House, built in 1781, was burnt down when the next door public house, the Kings Arms, caught fire.

In front of the Custom House stands the Town Beam which was used to weigh goods taken in and out of the town, the weight of goods was used to calculate the amounts of dues to be paid to pay for the dockworkers' wages and the upkeep of the quays.

The Ancient Ceremony of Beating of the Sea Bounds of Poole. Poole was granted its first charter from the Manor of Canford in 1248, and the boundaries were confirmed in the Winchelsea Certificate of 1364. The bounds where only beaten every 30 years or so, but since 1921 the boundaries have been checked systematically every few years in a historical reinactment of the Admiralty Court (abolished in 1836).

Left: The Mayor of Poole as Admiral of the Port reads the Winchelsea Certificate of 1365 and opens the Admiralty Court and swears in the Jury.

Top: The Jury led by the town mace bearer.

Above: the Mayor and Jury crossing to Hamworthy

Left: The Mayor, Herbert Carter, reading the Charter at "Broom Hill" Hamworthy in 1926.

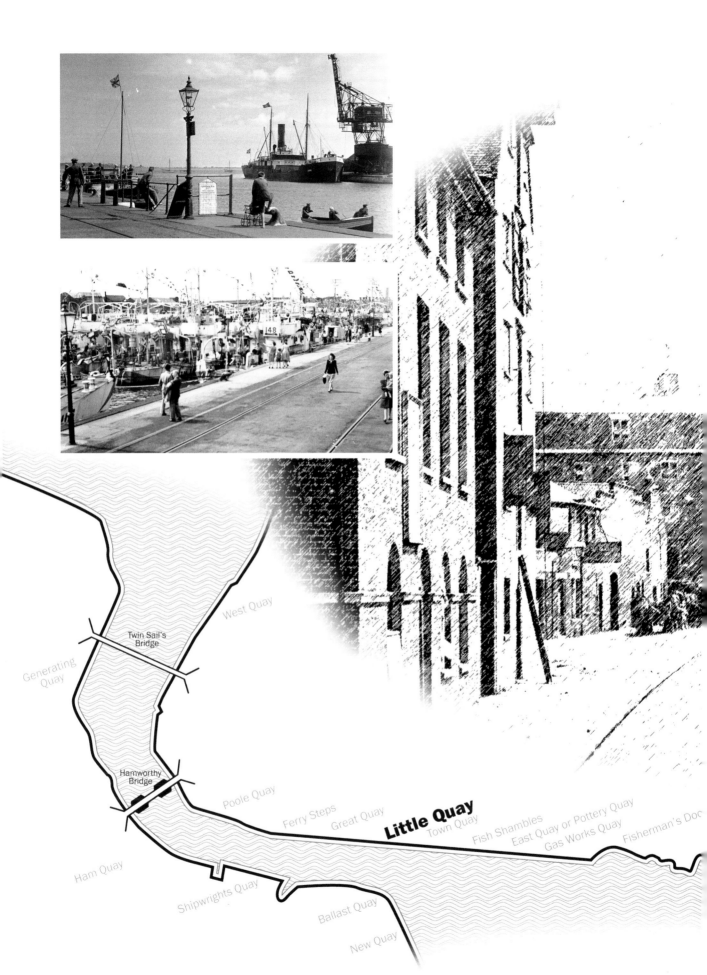

Twin Sail's Bridge

West Quay

Generating Quay

Hamworthy Bridge

Poole Quay

Ferry Steps

Great Quay

Little Quay

Town Quay

Fish Shambles

East Quay or Pottery Quay

Gas Works Quay

Fisherman's Doc

Ham Quay

Shipwrights Quay

Ballast Quay

New Quay

LITTLE QUAY

Baiter

This part of the Quay is named Little Quay. It was also known as the Gun Deck, into which the Quay Steps or "Quay Stairs" were built. A document states, in 1524 repairs were made to the wooden Gun Deck. This was a platform on which a number of guns were mounted on the quay front, which protected the Great Quay and the gateway to the town. The platform was the south gateway to the town and was ornamented with wooden lions, griffins and iron posts. The guns were kept ready loaded with a charge of gunpowder and pellets of lead and stone, kept dry by a cover. Spare powder and shot was kept in the loft of the Salisbury, a small prison behind the Town Cellar, ever ready to defend the town.

Left: A Company of French "Onion Johnnies" unloading a crop of onions imported from Roscoff in France. They were unloaded into carts to be stored in a local warehouse where they would string the onions up in the traditional way before selling them from their bicycles all over Dorset.

Top: Flags flying for Coronation day of King George VI on March 7th 1937

Above: 1935, a large crowd of people on the quayside watching the small boat tied up alongside. The Chimney in the background is at Yeatmans' Flour Mill.

Left: Oakley Bros. Corn Store 1951 - now Newfoundland House.

Ferry Steps. In medieval times it was from here people could catch small ferries to all parts of the Poole Harbour, it was well used because the roads were nonexistent or very poor and going by water was comfortable and faster.

About 1960, this ship was the largest ship to enter Poole Harbour; she was here to collect a cargo of Clay from Purbeck.

Poole Quay railway line was first laid from Poole Station in 1874 and was constructed level with West Quay Road and the Quay so that it did not hinder road traffic, apart from cyclists who often found themselves thrown off their bikes after steering into the track. The railway was well used until 1950 when ships became larger and no longer required to use the Poole railway link. This series of pictures was taken by Ivo Peters in 1954, many of his pictures also show his Bentley, NHY581.

Poole Quay Railway line ran the full length of West Quay road and into the south side of the Down Goods Siding at Poole Station. In the First World War most of the land to the north of West Quay Road was cleared and made into a marshalling yard. The engines were restricted to a speed of four miles an hour and a man carrying a red and green flags or a red light at night had to walk in front to warn people of the approaching train. By the early 1960's the trains and wagons were causing great traffic congestion in the town, because of people parking cars on the tracks. The last train ran 30th April 1960, and the line was later removed.

The Quay where it abuts Poole High Street. This area before the Quayside was built was an entrance way into the quay from High Street, known as Mesurer's Gap, it was like a slipway, where townspeople could bring their own boats to get access to the quay; the boats could be drawn up at high tide to be loaded, unloaded and repaired. Mesurer's Gap remained till 1618 when the New Quay and Fish Market Quay were built, known today as Town Quay.

The King's Arms was probably established here in the seventeenth century when Mesurer's Gap had been reclaimed. On the opposite side of the High Street is the Old Quay Tea House which was the Mariners' Arms, another very old Poole public House.

Above: The Quay from Hamside. The warehouse next to the Custom House was always known as "The White Warehouse"; being painted white it stood out from all the others.

Below: "PARKSTONE" of Poole owned by Carter's shipping agents.

When the railway trucks were left on the quay there was very little room left for pleasure boats to advertise their harbour trips. Before Brownsea Island opened to visitors in 1964, pleasure boats could only offer trips round Dorset Lakeland and Sandbanks, Shell Bay and, if the tide was right, to Wareham or to Bournemouth, Swanage and the Isle of Wight by paddle steamer.

Two unusual exports from Poole. Above: Probably about 1905, workmen are loading a sailing vessel with paving slabs probably brought over from Swanage as the vessel was the wrong shape to take the ground in Swanage Bay. Below: A Vessel loading scrap car and lorry tyres in the 1920's.

*An early
photograph of
Poole Quay
from the air,
showing ships
being broken
up after World
War One.*

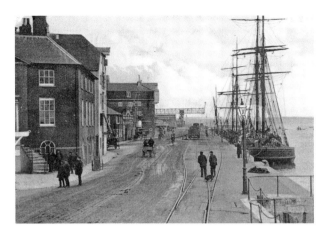

Top left: Local lads off to serve "King and Country" in the First World War.

Left: Divers repairing the Quay walls.

Below: General maintenance was always done in port.

Top: A captured German submarine U142 at Poole Quay January. 1919. She was a Type UB111 sold to the Japanese navy, served 1920 – 1921 and broken up in 1921 to become a floating jetty.

Left and below: "HMS POOLE" J147, on a courtesy visit to Poole Quay. She was a Bangor class minesweeper built in Glasgow in 1939, and scrapped in January 1948. She was based in the North Sea at Rosyth and used to ensure safe passage of convoys between the Thames Estuary and Scotland. She was the third ship to be named "HMS POOLE".

Above: A minesweeper built in Poole by Bolson's.

Top right: the Quay packed with US Coastguard Cutters taking on supplies before D-day.

Right: Motor torpedo ships moored off Poole Pottery.

Below: Fire-boat "FLAME" which patrolled the Quays in case of fire.

After the war, the ships used to free Europe returned to their ports of departure. Here the Quay is crowded with US Coastguard Cutters dressed overall celebrating the victory over Japan in the Far East.

"V.J. Day". Victory over Japan Day, on Poole Quay. These two pictures were taken on the day and evening of August 15th, 1945 the date on which the surrender of Japan occurred, formally ending World War Two.

For a week each year, from the late 1920's to the late 1940's Poole Harbour was turned into a small power boat race track. Boats were divided into classes and various courses were laid out in the harbour with pit stops and all the racing equipment like score boards and start lines etc.

At times some of the bigger classes were allowed to race like Hubert Scott-Paine, owner of the British Power Boat Company. "MISS BRITAIN 111" which achieved over 110 miles an hour,in 1934, on the waters of Poole Harbour, a record speed that has yet to be beaten.

The racing was, at the time, the only kind of boat racing on salt water, of this type in the country. The object of the race was to encourage development of motor boats and their engines. All the boats were standard ones as available to the public, so out-and-out racing machines and hydroplanes were barred. All parts had to be standard, off-the-shelf parts, and the boats had to be properly silenced. The picture (top left) shows the "FLORINDA", the then home of the Royal Motor Yacht Club being used to display the number of laps completed in the hundred mile race. The picture top right is the 715 ton steam yatch "MARION, owned by P.E. Shepherd, used by the RYMC as a floating HQ for the 1938 racing.

The course was four miles long and the race was for 25 laps a total length of 100 miles. The courses set up between the quays and under the bridge with turning buoys in the water off the Quay, with long straits or lanes, for high speeds in the channels off in the harbour, this giving spectators on the Quay plenty to see.

West Quay

Twin Sail's Bridge

Generating Quay

Hamworthy Bridge

Poole Quay

Ferry Steps

Great Quay

Little Quay

Town Quay

Fish Shambles

East Quay or Pottery Quay

Gas Works Quay

Fisherman's Dock

Ham Quay

Shipwrights Quay

Ballast Quay

New Quay

TOWN QUAY

Baiter

The Town Quay, originally named New Quay, was built in 1681. It was dominated by Belben's flour mill with the tall chimney. This was a landmark for shipping. In 1875 it was one of the very first steam-powered mills; it supplied flour all over southern England.

The Quay Steps on this part of the Quay are known as Custom House Steps as this was the nearest point that ships could berth to the Custom House to declare taxable goods.

Top: This grain unloading appliance used to unload bulk grain from a ship's hold, the straight tube into the hold enclosed a screw which raised the grain into the hopper.

Below: Alternatively, the ship's derricks and small quayside cranes were used to unload grain which was in sacks.

On 4th September 1727 the Mayor Benjamin Skutt ordered that a crane or "gin" - (an old word for lifting apparatus) should be erected on the quay for the unloading of goods and merchandise. This part of the Quay was used mostly for the handling of grain as most of the grain and seed warehouses were in this area although the Quay could be used for all sorts of cargo from timber to coal. After ships were unloaded the cargo still had to be transported by cart, lorry or by the railway to the other warehouses all round the town. Coal yards were mostly located all over the town, but the timber needed much larger areas for storage and was moved to large timber yards at West Quay or in Hamworthy and Parkstone.

Above: Away from the water's edge opposite the quay were storage warehouses and public houses, which gave the dockworkers, ship's crews and visitors refreshment.

Three pubs stood here next to each other, "Portsmouth Hoy", "Poole Arms" and, in between, the now closed "Britannia Inn".

Below: The brigantine "EMMA" from Viareggio Italy drying her sails on Town Quay in August 1928. She arrived in Poole early August 1928 from Biblao, Spain in ballast, and over the next two weeks loaded clay for the port of Civitavecchia, 50 miles North West of Rome.

Between each of these buildings and warehouses is an alley way. These alleyways were the jetties between the docks where the ships tied up to unload to the shore in Strand Street. In time the docks were filled in and the warehouses built and the jetties became the alleyways with the quay built in front of them.

This part of the Quay is known as Town Quay and it is the widest part of the Quay. Grain and seed was still the main cargo handled here, but it was also suitable for the larger cargos such as timber and railway track, as there was more room.

Above: This must have been a hot sunny day with a light wind, as all the ships have broken out the sails to dry them. They had to dry sails as often as possible as canvas soon rots if left damp and rolled up.

Stationary railway trucks were a common sight on the quay.

A train brought the full trucks of exports to the quay early each day. No full trucks were to be left on the quay overnight. In the daytime the full trucks were unloaded to ships, while empty trucks were loaded with imports. At the end of the day the train arrived again, took away the full trucks and rearranged the empty, ready for the next day.

The TS "ROYALIST" she is a regular visitor to Poole. She is a square rig brig owned and operated by the Marine Society & Sea Cadets. Her hull is 76 ft 6 in long, with an overall length of 96 ft 10 in. weighing 83 tons. As well as her sails, she is equipped with two Perkins diesel engines; the engines drive twin screw propellers.

"REGINA" is typical of the fleet trading schooners that, in the 19th century, as in the centuries before, would make the journey across the Atlantic each year to Newfoundland, taking out trade goods. They then loaded fish from the island, selling it in the Caribbean (where the vessel was reloaded with rum and sugar) or Mediterranean (where it was reloaded with fruit, wines and goods from the Far East trade routes) before returning to Poole.

The "RECORD REIGN" has the leeboards on her side probably because she was flat bottomed to take the ground in other European ports.

In Edwardian days there were few visitors to the Town Quay. It was a working place and could be quite dangerous for bystanders who did not understand the workings on the quay.

Town Quay, on a particularly busy day or when a larger cargo was expected, judging by the number of railway trucks.

Top: From Town Quay looking across to Hamside, The "MARIKA" with cranes unloading coal, to the coal yard on Ballast Quay.

Right: The "DROXFORD" of Southampton. She is a salvage and diving support vessel unloading a salvage cargo on New Quay, she was built 1958 and scrapped in 1980.

Above: Children sitting on the old wood deck quay, dated to around 1900. No health and safety regulations in those days!

Below: The Flying Angel, was the Missions to Seamen Church where ship's crew could find directions to good lodging with help and support. Piracy, shipwreck, abandonment and separation from loved ones are just a few of the problems seafarers face. Also it could provide a 'home away from home' for seafarers who may have been at sea for up to five years. It is now a restaurant.

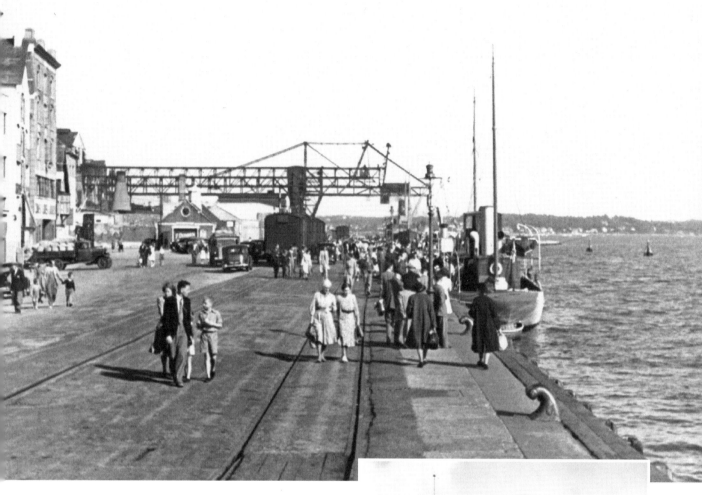

The Town Quay ends here, and the area known as the Fish Deck starts, as it was used mostly for landing of Fish from home and abroad.

West Quay

Twin Sail's
Bridge

Generating
Quay

Hamworthy
Bridge

Poole Quay

Ferry Steps

Great Quay

Little Quay

Town Quay

Fish Shambles

East Quay or Pottery Quay

Gas Works Quay

Fisherman's D

Ham Quay

Shipwrights Quay

Ballast Quay

New Quay

FISH
SHAMBLES

Baiter

The Jolly Sailor; this public house was first licensed to sell ale in 1785, and was rebuilt around 1890 to create the public house that fronts the Quay today.

Lord Nelson public house opened its doors as the Blue Boar Inn in about 1764, the house stands on reclaimed land as this area was a sea marsh and at high tide the area was under water.

Blue Boar Lane was the alleyway between the 'Jolly Sailor' and the 'Lord Nelson'. There were several tenements down this alleyway, popular with ship's crew as they could find board and lodging close to the public houses and the ships on the quay when in port.

Top: Poole Quay from the air c1920. The front row of buildings in the fourteenth century would have not been there as this area was sea marsh, and small jetties sticking out into deeper water.

The first Fish Shambles was built in 1830. It stood in the centre of the Quay known as the Fish Deck and is the area which the fishermen landed their catches to supply the inhabitants of Poole and surrounding area. In the 14th century there was a Fish Market House in Smack Alley believed to behind the present public houses.

All fish caught in the Poole area had to be offered to the local inhabitants in the Fish Shambles before it could be sold elsewhere.

A bell rung when the market opened and fish was available for sale, and it rang again at the close of the market.

Below: Poole fishermen showing off a catch of mackerel.

Bottom: Poole Fishermen outside the Fish Shambles in their 'Sunday Best' probably just before attending St James Church for the Annual Service of the Sea.

An Atlantic bluefin tuna, 9ft long and weighing around 650lb, found stranded on a mud bank in the harbour in 1896. It was displayed on a hand cart, and taken round the town.

The Fishermen later displayed it at Wade's grocer shop the back of the Electric Theatre.

Left to right: Mark Bolt, (he never wore shoes in summer), Mr. Biggs, Mr. Wade, Mr. George Brown, Mr. Thomas and Mr. Wills.

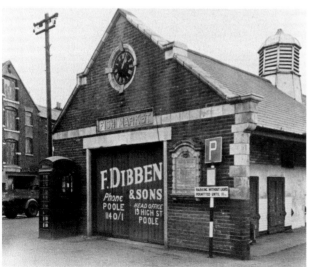

This Fish Shamble or Market opened in 1914, after the old round one was demolished because it was unhygienic. The market bell from the old shambles was incorporated into the new building. This building soon became redundant due to the loss of a great number of fishermen in the First World War and dwindling fish stocks. The building became a store and remained till 1959 when it was demolished. A new public shelter has now been built of a similar design to the original market shamble.

A donkey cart race on the Quay by Poole Fishermen. The picture was taken probably just before the First World War.

Below: In the summer months of the late 1950's and early 60's Poole children would earn pocket money by diving off the Quay for coins thrown into the water by passing holidaymakers.

Main picture: Before small boats offered trips 'Round the Harbour' the paddle steamers plied from the Fish Shambles Steps offering 'Trips Round the Bay' and rides to Bournemouth, Swanage, and Lulworth Cove.

Above: The Fish Deck was the widest part of the Quay all built on reclaimed land in the 1830's. Previously this area was shingle and seamarsh where the fisherman landed their catch and hauled out their boats for repair and maintenance.

Left: The Poole fishing fleet alongside the Quay unloading sprats or herring. Both fish were plentiful in Poole Bay in the autumn.

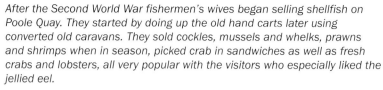

After the Second World War fishermen's wives began selling shellfish on Poole Quay. They started by doing up the old hand carts later using converted old caravans. They sold cockles, mussels and whelks, prawns and shrimps when in season, picked crab in sandwiches as well as fresh crabs and lobsters, all very popular with the visitors who especially liked the jellied eel.

Center left: Mr. Matthews selling fresh fish at Fisherman's Dock.

Top Above: Tom Hockey, fish seller, outside old library in Lagland Street. He was said to have the loudest voice in Poole. There is a story that he was brought before the magistrates for shouting "Mackerel" out too loudly. He won his case as he told the magistrate he could not say "M" so he was shouting "Ackerel"!

Above: Harry Beale Poole fish merchant. He pushed his cart all round the town and to Wimborne three times a week.

Left: Mrs. Neta Brimicombe wife of Poole fisherman "Pompey" selling cockles, cigarette in hand!

The shellfish stalls became illegal after the passing of a local Act of Parliament in 1961, and all fish sales had to be from hygienic purpose built buildings.

Main picture: A Hythe-Class "Superbird" Flying-Boat in 1946, with mechanics servicing the engines. Note the female crew, on the tender, attending the mooring.

Above: Pilots and cabin staff preparing to leave

Left: Red Cross food parcels destined for prisoners of war. Stewardesses loading vacuum flasks of drinking water required for the long flights.

Poole was the UK's only International Airport and link to the commonwealth from 1938, through the war, to 1947. BOAC set up operations and Poole Pottery was used as the terminal for passengers and crew were shipped from the Quay to the waiting planes which used the Main Channel as a runway.

Main picture: Two BOAC Sunderland Flying Boats at their moorings.

Mooring Crew at their duties and loading mail and cargo on the Quay.

Paddle Steamers have been part of life on Poole Quay since the 1850's. In the early days they were used as tug boats to move cargo barges around the port, to tow larger sailing ships in and out of the harbour, and taking people out on pleasure trips.

Top: Poole Tug 'TELEGRAPH' was one of the first Poole Paddle Steamers. When not required for towing she did passenger trips to Bournemouth, Swanage and occasionally to Lulworth and Weymouth.

Bottom left: The 'MONARCH' a twin funnelled ship started in Poole in 1888 and continued till 1946 sailing mostly to Bournemouth and Swanage as well as passages to the Channel Isles and France.

The 'MONARCH II' constructed in 1924 came to Poole in 1951 as a replacement for the 'MONARCH', she ran a regular service to Swanage and Bournemouth till 1960 with the 'PRINCESS ELIZABETH'.

The "LORD ELGIN" came to Poole in 1881 and became a favourite with locals and visitors, making regular trips to Sandbanks and Swanage. She later went on to become the Southampton to Cowes cargo ferry, she was the last cargo carrying paddle steamer in 1955.

"SWANAGE QUEEN" built in 1927, came to Poole in 1961 as a replacement for the "MONARCH" but by this time continental holidays were all the vogue and because of her poor takings the service was discontinued and she was scrapped in the next year.

The "STUDLAND BELL", A small paddler that was able to go to places the larger ones could not, she did regular trips to Sandbanks, Studland and when the tide allowed up the river to Wareham

The "EMPEROR OF INDIA", built in 1906, arrived in Poole in 1908. She was able to do longer passages to the Isle of Wight, Weymouth and in high summer to Cherbourg, France.

The "BOURNEMOUTH".

The "EMBASSY".

The "MAJESTIC".

The "LORD ELGIN".

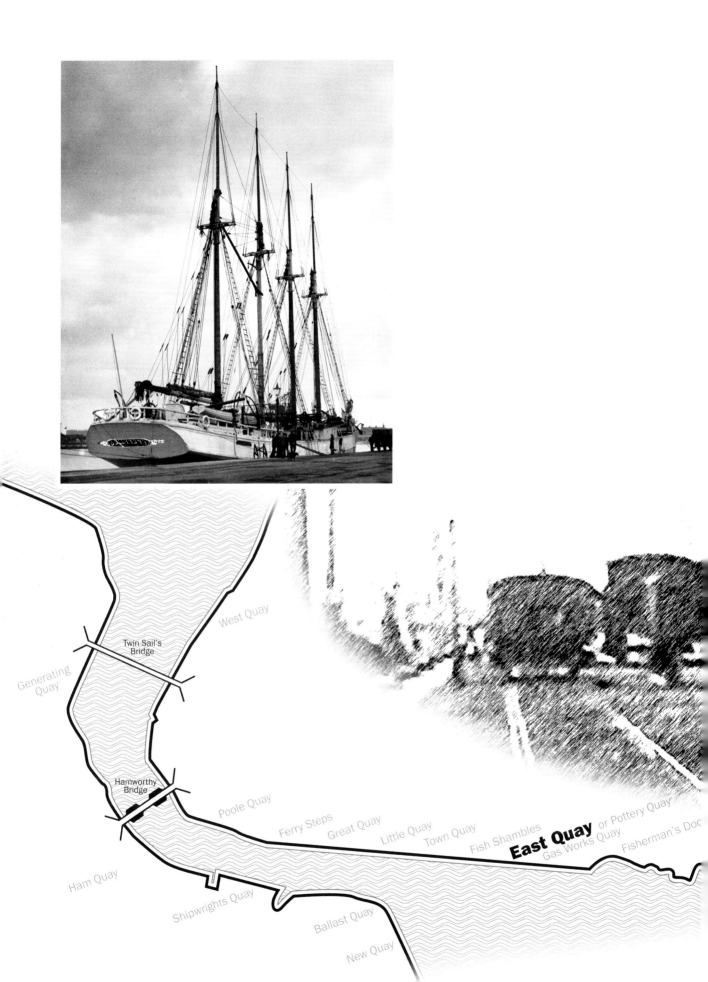

West Quay

Twin Sail's
Bridge

Generating
Quay

Hamworthy
Bridge

Poole Quay

Ferry Steps

Great Quay

Little Quay

Town Quay

Fish Shambles

East Quay or Pottery Quay

Gas Works Quay

Fisherman's Doc

Ham Quay

Shipwrights Quay

Ballast Quay

New Quay

EAST QUAY
or Pottery Quay

Baiter

In the 1800's before the sea wall was built round Fisherman's Dock, the Poole fishing fleet anchored on moorings in the area known as Oyster bank.

Oyster bank was formed by fishermen cleaning their catch of Poole oysters and other shellfish from their boats at the end of a fishing trip. All the waste was thrown overboard thus forming the bank. Catches were plentiful and oysters a common and cheap diet. Many of the buildings on the older quays are built on similar banks of oyster shells.

Bottom left: Before Poole Pottery was built in the early 1900's the unused land, owned by Mr.Bankes, of Kingston Lacy, was used by fishermen to dry nets. East Quay Road was then the shore boundary.

Bottom right: Richard Wills, a retired Poole Lifeboat Coxswain, mending his nets on Poole Quay.

Above: Poole Quay Lime Kiln was erected on East Quay in 1871, Lime was used in Poole since the earliest times and was used as a stabilizer in mud walls and floors. The kiln was built here because of the easy access to limestone from the Purbeck Hills and the availability of coal from the ships importing it. The kiln was destroyed in a fire.

Below: A few years later and another five kilns have been built and fired for Carters Poole Pottery, founded in 1873

East Quay or Pottery Quay also now named by marketing managers as Dolphin Quays. Above as it was laid with the railway lines and below, the railway lines have been removed in the 1960's and was then used as a general cargo area and cars could park when it was not in use.

Pottery has been made in Poole and Dorset for centuries. What is known as The Poole Pottery today on Poole Quay started when a brick and tile pottery started up next to the old Lime Kiln and the fishermen's drying ground. In 1873 Jesse Carter took over and started to make architectural fire clay goods and tiles, later producing decorative lustreware.

Above: The northern boundary of Poole Pottery is along East Quay Road, the three storey building is the original brick works.

Right: Poole Pottery from the Quayside with the distinctive tiles on the wall.

In the 1960's Poole handled large cargoes of grain which were exported from the UK. This grain handling plant was built on the Quay and could take several loaded lorries and store the grain in the silos, until the ship arrived to take on the cargo, The turnaround time of the ship was quite short, making grain handling in Poole quite competitive compared with other ports. The apparatus could also be reversed and grain could be sucked out of ships into the silo and the loaded into lorries for transport to other grain silos and stores around the town.

A row of rail trucks loaded with coal and a fleet of lorries
waiting to load coal which is being loaded into sacks.

The "HINRICH PETERS" of Hamburg in the 1930's with a
cargo of timber, flying the German Swastika flag.

Another large import of timber
to Poole is being unloaded,
ready to be transported to the
local timber yards. Timber was
in demand in the area due to
the rapid pace of house
building.

Steamers alongside the Quay.

"SHIFTER" was a harbour tug. She was used to move the Poole Harbour Board dredger. and a fleet of three dumb barges "HOP" "SKIP" & "JUMP". The fleet was used to keep the Quays and the Harbour channels clear of mud and sand. When the dredger had filled one of the barges the tug took them all out to sea, as neither the dredger nor the dumb barges had engines.

When they reached the spoil ground off Old Harry, the doors in the bottom were opened to dump the contents on the spoil ground in deep water.

Right: An usually large (for Poole) fourmasted sailing ship, the Italian "GULLAROMA" at the Pottery Quay, being the deepest end of all the quays.

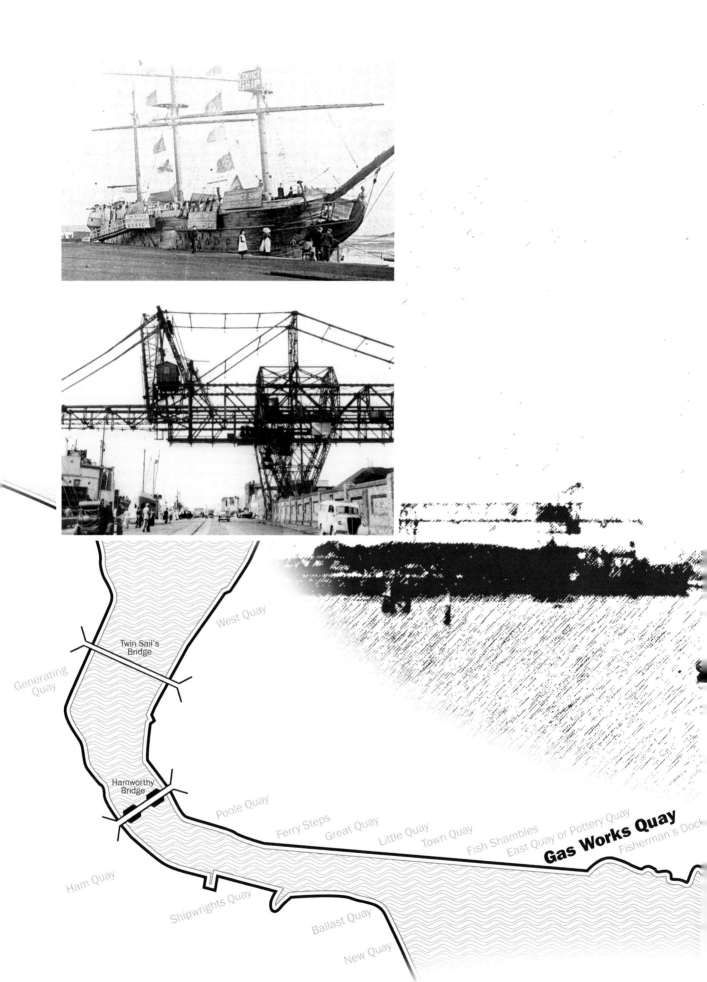

West Quay

Twin Sail's
Bridge

Generating
Quay

Hamworthy
Bridge

Poole Quay

Ferry Steps   Great Quay   Little Quay   Town Quay   Fish Shambles   East Quay or Pottery Quay   **Gas Works Quay**   Fisherman's Dock

Ham Quay

Shipwrights Quay

Ballast Quay

New Quay

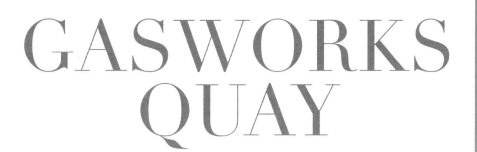

GASWORKS QUAY

Baiter

The "C.&F. NURSE", a two-masted topsail schooner built in 1900 for Nurse Bros. of Bridgwater. She carried mixed cargoes between the UK and continental ports.

The Russian ship setting sails ready to leave after unloading at Gas Works Quay.

From Pottery Quay looking down to Gas Works Quay.

Above: Gas Works Quay from the air.

Below: The Poole and Swanage Lifeboats off the Quay, possibly in a joint exercise, with the coal transporter in the background.

In 1902 the Quays were extended again to create a coal handling plant to supply the Gas Works with cheap sea transported coal. Two transporters were built the first had a capacity of 50 tons per hour and it was so successful a second was built this one could handle 100 tons an hour. The coal was lifted from the ship's hold and traversed across the coal storage ground. When both transporters were working a cargo of 1,100 tons could be unloaded in ten hours.

When completed it became the largest coal transporter in the British Isles, 283ft long and 56ft high, the Grab lifts 20 hundredweight in each lift, and the whole apparatus can be operated by one man and a series of hoppers and chain buckets conveying coal into the retort. An aerial coal cableway took coal across to the Pitwines site. Children and poor families would scavenge any coal that fell out on the quay and surrounding streets for use in their own hearths.

The four masted sailing ship "WESTWARD" off Gas Works Quay. She was in Poole to be converted to a hotel ship with the intention of mooring her in the harbour in the 1930's.

The Temperley Transporter Conveyor for loading and unloading coal. At first there was only one with a 33 ton an hour capacity. The Transporter Conveyor proved so successful another the Mitchell Transporter was built alongside (see opposite page). This was installed in 1922, with a capacity of 100 tons per hour. This enabled a ship to have two holds unloaded at the same time, or unload two ships at the same time.

Bucket conveyors extended for a length of 1,250 feet linking Pitwines Gas Works, supplying coal and returning coke ???? flying over the roofs of intervening buildings. The gasworks then employed about 1,000 people.

The deep water channel of the Gas Works Quay was not easy for ships to navigate as there was no space available to turn round, so all ships had to be manoeuvred with the aid of a Tug boat. This was the job of the "WENDY ANN" tugs.

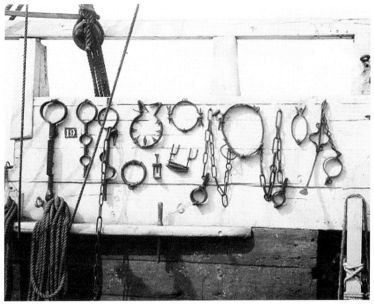

Above: A selection of torture or iron tools used onboard convict ships.

Convict Ship "SUCCESS" on Poole Quay, c1897. She was formerly a merchant ship and Australian convict hulk, refitted as a museum convict ship.

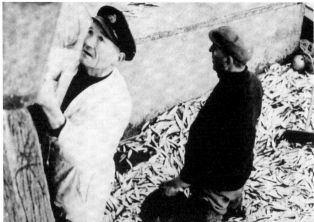

Sprats ussually arrive in Poole Bay in great quantities around Christmas time. Poole fishermen had special large nets which they used to catch the whole shoal and because of the size of the net it needed two boats to tow it. A good catch meant the two boats could be loaded to the gunwales, almost to a point where they would capsize. Sometimes they caught more they could be taken home, and this resulted in them calling in other boats to take the rest of the catch.

When the sprats were brought to the Quay they had to be unloaded, 1981/2 was a particularly good season, the best and largest sprats were boxed up and sent to markets all over the country whilst the smaller fish were bagged up to be used as fertilizer on the fields around Poole. The weather was particularly cold that year and great piles of frozen sprats were piled up on the Quay.

PE 25

H&A BURDEN

FITTERS

Generating
Quay

West Quay

Twin Sail's
Bridge

Hamworthy
Bridge

Poole Quay

Ferry Steps

Great Quay

Little Quay

Town Quay

Fish Shambles

East Quay or Pottery Quay

Gas Works Quay

Fisherma

Ham Quay

Shipwrights Quay

Ballast Quay

New Quay

FISHERMAN'S DOCK

Baiter

When the Quays were built on the land which was to become Poole Pottery and the Gasworks, the fishermen lost their traditional land where they had kept their boats. A piece of land which was owned by Henry Bankes of Kingston Lacy estate was gifted to the fishermen so they could have a new drying area to dry nets and pull their boats out. A protected area for the boats was built off the shore by constructing a wooden stake wall; this was later replaced by a rock sea wall. At the same time a new lifeboat house was built with a slipway alongside to launch the lifeboat. The Gasworks also used the quayside to provide cooling water to the works. the distinctive building was the pump house.

Before the First World War all the fishing boats were either powered by sail or with oars, including the lifeboat. The picture above shows the dock before the war and, below, after the war when war surplus lorry engines became available and the fishermen installed them in their boats.

Opposite: It looks as if these young urchins loved standing on the dock railings taking in the life on the quayside. Generations of children have enjoyed watching life below the water. This wall was an excellent place as the light conditions allowed you to see clearly though the water's surface to admire the sea life below.

A lot of the time spent fishing was taken up by repairs to boats and gear. Nets needed regular repair as cotton nets were not as strong as today's nylon and they needed to be dried regularly to stop the rot setting in if allowed to remain wet. Poole has a variety of shellfish to be caught such as, crabs, lobsters, prawns, cockles, mussels and oysters. The fish mostly flatfish, plaice and flounders, with mullet, bass and eels are in abundance. In winter large shoals of sprats and herring come into the area. Salmon and trout are also to be had when the fish are making their way to their spawning grounds in the rivers Frome and Piddle which emptied into the harbour.

Top: Cleaning, drying nets and repairing them are still a large part of fishing.

Below: Richard Hayes, ex coxswain of Poole Lifeboat, cleaning and mending his nets.

Left: Bill Hayes, a Poole pilot. Bill was also second coxswain on the Lifeboat.

Right: 'Cannot' Charley Stephens inspecting the dry nets.

Centre: Ben Pond a fisherman who kept to the south side of the Harbour in his double ended Poole Canoe "TAM".

Bottom: Henry Matthews in a traditional double-end Poole Canoe which was light enough to skim over the mudflats.

Eels are another plentiful fish in Poole Harbour, and they can be caught all over the harbour especially in the soft muddy areas. They live in holes burrowing in the mud. The fishermen had a special flat pronged spear which they could thrust down into the mud and any eels hiding there could be caught between the prongs. Two favourite places to catch eels are Poole Park and the Blue Lagoon.

Opposite far left: Albert Brown, Poole fisherman and coxswain of Poole lifeboat 1946 – 1948, standing; he is talking to Richard Cartridge, another Poole fisherman.

Opposite left: Skipper of "STARFISH" Tom Brown with a large skate, and Sir Henry Page Croft, 1st Baron Croft, M.P. for Bournemouth 1918 - 1940.

Below left: Skipper of "STARFISH" Tom Brown and a client with a selection of sharks and skate.

The Poole Fishermen's Band an entry to Poole carnival, lead by the lifeboat Coxswain. The instruments came from Mr. Charles Van Raalte on Brownsea Island.

'Curly' Greenslade, showing off a fine 12lbs. Lobster.

Peter Matthews with a large cock crab.

Above: When the tram shelter at Brown Bottom (Poole Civic Centre) became redundant, it was re-erected on the fishermen's drying ground to provide shelter. Unfortunately it suffered from lack of maintenance and vandalism, and it eventually became a support for the November the 5th bonfire that the children built each year to celebrate Guy Fawkes. This fire also cleared a large amount of rubbish from around the town.

Below: The fishing boat hard and Ballard Road.

Right: The building in the distance is the watch keeper's home in front of a large pumping station, which kept Old Town Poole clear of surface water and sewerage until replaced by a new one at the end of High Street, capped by the Caro sculpture 'Sea Music'.

Fishermen's Regatta, showing the race for the larger Poole motor fishing boats. They started at Hamworthy Bridge and raced down to Aunt Betty Buoy (about half way down the harbour) and back to the finishing line off the Custom House.

All the boats in this race had engines, and they were allowed to use sails and oars to increase speed. There were other races for rowing boats and boats towing a trawl, with prizes for the most fish caught.

Left: Alongside the Lifeboat house is one of the few public slipways into the harbour and is today the only one left on the Quay as all the previous ones are now quayside. When the Lifeboat House was first built the lifeboat was on a wheeled carriage which was kept in the house and when needed it was wheeled out and launched down this slipway or taken down to Baiter to be launched there. Later the Lifeboat House was redesigned and given its own slipway and the carriage removed.

Above: The Crew of the Poole Lifeboat "CITY MASONIC CLUB" about 1920. The Coxswain, in the cap, is Richard Wills.

Below: The Lifeboat House now a Museum holding the former Poole Lifeboat the "THOMAS KIRK WRIGHT".

Opposite top: The Poole Lifeboat Crew in the Lifeboat "CITY MASONIC CLUB".

Opposite bottom: Launching day of the lifeboat "HARMER" June 1910.

Above: The newly named lifeboat "HARMER" coming down the slipway for the first time. Inset: Dick Hayes lighting the maroon to muster the crew.

Below: The "HARMER" and her crew on the slipway.

Top: The "HARMER" being rowed by her crew coming into Fisherman's Dock.

Above and below: The Poole Lifeboat the "THOMAS KIRK WRIGHT" launching from the lifeboat house.

The Fishermen's Drying Ground was the only open space in this part of town and it was regularly used for people to gather together. Here they have come to listen to Freddy Guest electioneering in his quest to become MP for Poole in 1910.

Above: Beyond the Gas Works is the spit of land named Baiter. It was used as a burial ground for victims of plague and the Black Death of the 14th century. One of the town's Windmills was also built here. Lying outside the town the gallows were also sited on Baiter

Pitwines Gasworks was built at the edge of the old town. Here the coal that was unloaded at the Quay was turned into town gas by heating it up in a retort and treating it in a condenser to remove the gas and tar, at the same time turning the coal to coke that could still be used as smoke free fuel.

The remains of the first Poole Swimming Baths, in 1960, built on the harbour shore off the southern end of Green Road. The pool was fed by warm water from the cooling process at the gasworks, it had two changing rooms for male and female swimmers and because of the warm water it was very popular with the town's people who at the time had no baths at home. Because it was on the shore it had problems with stones and sand coming into it from the harbour.

Below: Is the 1786 Powder House which had to be used to store gunpowder from ships moored at the Quay. The roof survived untill the mid 1950's, but now only the foundations are visible. A project for its restoration is under discussion.

Below right: The Isolation Hospital where ships' crew who arrived ill from foreign ports could be isolated to prevent the spreading of infectious diseases such as cholera or smallpox around the town.

66 Beside the ever breezy sea,
This Ancient Town of Poole doth stand;
Where tan fishing nets are drying,
Hung on old stone quay.
And rattling cranes are winding
The coal above you see 99

B Eves 1928